A Walk Thru the Book of

JONAH

Experiencing God's Relentless Grace

Walk Thru the Bible

BakerBooks

a division of Baker Publishing Group
Grand Rapids, Michigan

Published by Baker Books
a division of Baker Publishing Group
P.O. Box 6287, Grand Rapids, MI 49516-6287
www.bakerbooks.com

Printed in the United States of America

Library of Congress Cataloging-in-Publication Data
A walk thru the book of Jonah : experiencing God's relentless grace / Walk Thru the Bible.
   p. cm.
   Includes bibliographical references.
   ISBN 978-0-8010-7171-3 (pbk.)
   1. Bible. O.T. Jonah—Study and teaching. 2. Bible. O.T. Jonah—Criticism, interpretation, etc. I. Walk Thru the Bible (Educational ministry).
BS1605.55.W36 2009
224′.920071—dc22   2008050829

Cover image: resonants / iStock

Contents

Introduction

In the beginning, God created the heavens and the earth. Sometime after that beginning, however, humanity managed to thrust his creation back into disorder. Ever since, God has sought to redeem. And he has been relentless too. The Bible is a record of his constant calling, his great love for those who need him, his jaw-dropping sacrifice that still causes men and angels to bow down in awe.

The book of Jonah is one example among many of God's relentless pursuit of those who will turn to him. It has connotations of Genesis 1: the tumultuous deep over which the Spirit brooded, for example; as well as hints of Revelation 22—a vast city that, at least for a moment in time, becomes pure in heart and completely devoted to him. In some respects, it's a portrait of redemptive history: Jonah represents the nation of Israel reluctantly fulfilling its calling to be a light to the world; and Nineveh is the lost Gentile masses that are inexplicably drawn to their Creator's word. And beneath the drama is the pounding, pleading heart of God that longs to pour out its mercy.

Jonah is an unusual book. It's one among the collection of twelve minor prophets, but it doesn't read like any of the rest. For one thing, the other prophetic books were written by the prophets or their scribes. Jonah is a third-person story of the prophet himself. Moreover, the story reads like history in some parts and fiction in others—which, along with the highly unusual fish predicament, causes some to consider the prophecy a parable or allegory. But parables and allegories generally don't designate the main character by an identifiable time and place (the son of Amittai from Gath-Hepher). And the Son of God himself referred to Jonah as one would speak of a historical figure (Matt. 12:41).

Regardless of the enigmatic nature of the story, Jonah packs powerful messages on obedience, prejudice, compassion, bitterness, and God's mission to the nations of the world. A reader who comes to grip with Jonah's truths will come face to face with a relentless God of grace.

The Prophet and His Times

The Bible mentions Jonah ben Amittai only once outside of the book of Jonah: in 2 Kings 14:25, where he is said to have prophesied an expansion of Israel's territory (as had Elisha in the previous chapter) during the reign of Jeroboam II. That dates Jonah's ministry at around the middle of the eighth century BC, a time when Assyria and its capital Nineveh were a serious threat and a viable enemy, but a generation before Assyrian king Shalmanezer sacked the northern kingdom of Israel in 722 BC and Sennacherib brutalized parts of Judea in 701 BC. At the time of Jonah, Assyria was an intimidating foe on the verge of growing much more intimidating.

Jonah is a prophet from Gath-hepher in the region of Galilee—a fact the Pharisees conveniently ignored in one of their criticisms of Jesus (John 7:52). Traditionally, some rabbinic commentators have identified him as the son of the widow of Zarephath whom Elijah raised from the dead—an interesting thought, and chronologically possible, but with no biblical evidence.

We can assume from Jonah's only other recorded prophecy that he thought in terms of restoring Israel to its former glory under Solomon. In his mind, this defined the mission of God. And there were other prophecies to that effect. This was God's revealed will. Israel would one day rise up and defeat her enemies, and God would be glorified in his victory. As we'll see, the message he's told to preach to Nineveh goes radically against this grain.

The Book

No one knows exactly who recorded the events of Jonah into a book or when it was written. It's remotely possible that the prophet wrote it himself, but if so, he must have developed a radical humility since his Nineveh episode. The picture it paints isn't flattering in the least; only a dramatically changed man could have written with such self-incriminating honesty. A reference to Nineveh in the past tense (3:3) has led some to suggest that the book was written by a scribe after the destruction of Nineveh in 612 BC, but the past tense could simply refer to how large Nineveh was when Jonah went there. Regardless, the dramatic example of Gentiles repenting, the heavy emphasis on God's compassion for those who repent, and the stubbornness of one of Israel's own prophets all seem to indicate a strong motive for the writer. The book is a message urging God's people to turn away from wickedness and toward their compassionate God before his judgment falls. It could, therefore, have been written soon after Jonah's ministry but shortly before Assyria conquered Israel and dispersed the ten northern tribes. It serves as that kind of warning for God's people.

How to Use This Guide

The questions in this guide are geared to elicit every participant's input, regardless of his or her level of preparation. Obviously, the more group members prepare by reading the biblical text and the background information in the study guide, the more they will get out of it. But even in busy weeks that afford no preparation time, everyone will be able to participate in a meaningful way.

The discussion questions also allow your group quite a bit of latitude. Some groups prefer to briefly discuss the questions in order to cover as many as possible, while others focus only on one or two of them in order to have more in-depth conversations. Since this study is designed for flexibility, feel free to adapt it according to the personality and needs of your group.

Each session ends with a hypothetical situation that relates to the passage of the week. Discussion questions are provided, but group members may also want to consider role-playing the scenario or setting up a two-team debate over one or two of the questions. These exercises often cultivate insights that wouldn't come out of a typical discussion.

Regardless of how you use this material, the biblical text will always be the ultimate authority. Your discussions may take you to many places and cover many issues, but they will have the greatest impact when they begin and end with God's Word itself. And never forget that the Spirit who inspired the Word is in on the discussion too. May he guide it—and you—wherever he wishes.

Jonah is from Galilee
Jonah was a minor prophet

Mission Impossible

JONAH 1

Imagine being called by God to stand in Red Square during the height of the Cold War and shout out his judgment against communism. It would be no easy task or really even a sensible one. Even the most zealous mission agencies would advise against it. The only predictable result would be your imprisonment or worse. And if you weren't in the mood to die just yet, you might flee the call.

It's easy to criticize Jonah in retrospect. After all, it was the almighty God of the universe who told him to go. Did he really think God might not know what he was doing? He's the same God who had called Moses to go to Egypt so many centuries before, which worked out pretty well, and the same

9

God who had promised to take care of those who love and obey him. Still, we all know that God defines our welfare differently than we do. He has allowed many of his faithful servants to be martyrs. And few believers are really interested in being the next one.

Perhaps it's so easy for us to broad-brush Jonah as a coward because the writer of his story seems to do the same. The prophet does not come across favorably in his own book. But his dilemma was real, and while most of us don't run in the opposite direction from God, we do tend to ignore him quite often. Perhaps his will is too unpleasant or threatening to our own agenda, or perhaps we just don't listen very well. Or maybe we've assumed that conforming to his character or following his guidance is, more often than not, impossible. But God doesn't normally call us to do the possible. He searches the hearts of his people to find those who are willing to take on impossibili-

A SAVAGE REPUTATION

Assyria had a reputation for ruthless atrocities: skinning victims alive, pulling out their tongues, stacking heads into monstrous mounds, torturing and mutilating victims, and so on. This was, to be fair, in a much different historical context than ours—even many of Israel's kings were known to brutalize their enemies. But Assyria in particular seems to have mastered the art of psychological terrorism by prominently displaying its victims.

Much of Assyria's reputation was earned after the time of Jonah during the overthrow of the ten northern tribes and subsequent incursions into Judah and Egypt. But the character of its dynasties didn't spring up overnight; it evolved over time, including Jonah's. So when the prophet was told to go to Nineveh, the terror was, even then, probably very real.

ties by heroic faith—people who, in spite of their inclinations, refuse to run the other way.

Fugitive from God: Jonah 1:1–3

When the word of the Lord comes to Jonah regarding Nineveh, he has probably already prophesied to King Jeroboam about Israel's expansion, a restoration of territories that belonged to Solomon a century earlier but were later taken by Syria. He likely expects this national expansion to continue, perhaps all the way to Nineveh. After all, God is able, and he has promised to establish Israel as a strong and everlasting kingdom. That's a message a prophet like Jonah can get behind. But the preservation of an enemy? That's another story. This new message seems so unlike the flavor of his earlier ministry. Jonah wants nothing to do with the un-chosen people far from the land of promise.

So he immediately heads to Joppa on the Mediterranean shore. Nineveh is east, across the Tigris River from modern-day Mosul, Iraq. Joppa and the Mediterranean—and the very distant port of Tarshish (likely in Spain)—are west. And Jonah doesn't just find a ship and pay his own way. Some rabbinic commentators think the Hebrew text implies a full charter of the entire ship, cargo and all. Why? Perhaps he doesn't want it to wait in port for more cargo before leaving, or maybe he wants to ensure that the ship can't be redirected to a closer port without his permission. Regardless, he wants to dictate the terms of departure: to leave soon and stay gone for a very long time.

Because Nineveh is a far distance away already, Jonah could disobey simply by refusing to move from where he is. That's what most disobedience looks like. So why does he run in the opposite direction to get farther away? Probably he assumes that the prophetic voice is quieter—much less active and intrusive—

JONAH RAN

Jonah did what no other prophet in Scripture is said to have done: he blatantly disobeyed a command of God. There were certainly other reluctant prophets—Moses, for example, who argued with the voice from a burning bush in Exodus 3, and Jeremiah, whose calling made him miserable—but Jonah actually turned the other way and bolted. But God, who has always had plenty of resources (human and otherwise) at his disposal, didn't go searching for someone else. He gave Jonah the same command after the fish episode (3:1), demonstrating a truth Paul articulated years later: "God's gifts and his call are irrevocable" (Rom. 11:29). This time, Jonah obeyed. God's calling was an offer he couldn't refuse—literally.

outside the Promised Land. The further away someone is from God's temple and his people, the less likely that person might be to get sucked into divine activity. Or so he thinks.

Discuss

- Has God ever asked the impossible of you? How did you respond?

  _____

  _____

- If you were in a situation in which you were faced with enemies on a national scale, would you be more concerned with how they could be defeated or how they could turn to God? Which solution seems more likely? Which seems more effective? Why?

  _____

  _____

  _____

The Sleeper: Jonah 1:4–17

The Lord himself sends a violent storm against the ship, and the religiously diverse crew cries out to a variety of gods. Apparently, no god seems to be answering. But one man is strangely asleep in the bowels of the boat, which means there's a deity not being petitioned. Just in case that deity happens to matter, the captain rouses the patron of this journey.

The sailors' divination points to Jonah as the problem, and the prophet gives all the right answers. He worships the only true Lord, the God who made heaven, earth, and sea, the One who could put a stop to the raging waters with just a whisper of a word. So why has this sleeper run away from such a powerful God and provoked his anger? No answer is given. But this isn't a time for explanations anyway. The better question is what to do to calm the sea. And the answer to that is calm and decisive: "Pick me up and throw me into the sea" (1:12).

These are honorable Gentiles, though—more concerned for human life than God's prophet is, apparently—so they try to row to shore instead. The storm only rages harder. Then these idolaters call out to the God of Israel for their lives and ask forgiveness for what they are about to do: throw a man overboard. And astonishingly, the sea grows calm. The men fear God and make offerings and vows to him. Even in his apathy and self-focus, the prophet has turned rebellious hearts to the Lord.

The sovereign God who sent the storm now sends a fish. And Jonah spends three days in darkness.

Discuss

- If you were to ignore God's guidance, do you think he would find someone else or repeat his call until you obeyed? Why?

_____

_____

_____

_____

A CASE STUDY

Imagine: It's the middle of the night, and you've just been awakened from a deep sleep by a voice in your ear. There's no need to ask who it is. You know. Its unmistakable clarity and its overwhelming authority draw out such depths of awe in you—it has to be God. The voice is full of compassion too, and it's giving you an assignment: go at once to the city of Mecca and walk through its streets boldly proclaiming the way of Jesus.

- Which would impact you more profoundly: the divine encounter or the prospect of a sudden and violent death? Why?
- What do you think friends and relatives would say about the voice? What would they advise you to do?
- In all honesty, how do you think you would respond to your dilemma—emotionally and practically?

Three Dark Days

JONAH 2

Reverend Dimmesdale's health was slowly eroding. He had covered up his sin for years, and now it was catching up with him. Concealing his immoral affair for so long had weighed on him so heavily that he even sought out opportunities to confess it—to God, to the town, to anyone who needed to know. Anything, even the shame, would be better than holding on to the secret because secrets are heavy burdens. This one had to come out.

That was the inner turmoil of the pastor in Nathaniel Hawthorne's *The Scarlet Letter.* The esteemed minister had impregnated the main character, and for years she wore the scarlet A for "adultery" while he kept his ministry and his reputation intact. But guilt has a way of ravaging a life. As David wrote,

17

THE DESCENT OF DISOBEDIENCE

With literary flair, the original language of the story graphically describes Jonah's descent. He's literally told to *arise* and go to Nineveh in 1:2, but in 1:3, he goes *down* to Joppa, where he then goes *down* into the ship. In 1:5, he goes *down* into the inner part of the ship, where he lies *down* to sleep. From there, a fish takes him *down* into the depths of the sea, which Jonah acknowledges in extreme terms in 2:6. This, of course, is more than a spatial descent. It's the downward spiral of disobedience—the only direction to go when one runs from God. The good news is that with God's people, what goes down must come up. The captain of the ship tells Jonah to get *up,* the sailors pick him *up* to throw him into the sea, and the fish vomits him *up* onto dry land. Interestingly, Jonah directly or indirectly initiated every downward step, while someone else initiated each upward movement—not a bad picture of how grace works in our lives.

keeping sin a secret can cause a body to waste away under the weight. The cost of a cover-up is almost always greater than its benefit. Sin destroys from within.

Perhaps that's how Jonah felt as he sailed away from his calling. He slept in the bottom of a boat in the midst of a raging storm—much like a Savior centuries later but for completely different reasons. Some think Jonah was simply oblivious to his situation or relieved that he was successfully avoiding God's onerous call, but it's just as likely that he was trying to cover his sin, growing depressed, apathetic, and lethargic, and becoming genuinely unconcerned whether he or anyone else lived or died. Guilt will do that to a person. Burdens of conscience create restlessness, which exaggerates stress, which overloads a mind and a body with its weight, which ultimately paralyzes whoever is trying to bear the guilt in the first place. And Jonah acted just like someone who was paralyzed.

We know when we've disobeyed God, even when that knowledge is only a restless feeling deep within. We may deny that it's real guilt—we're great at rationalizing our disobedience. When we are at odds with him, the Spirit and the conscience he gave us will let us know. If we try to cover it up, the guilt will only grow stronger. The only remedy is to confess to the God of mercy and trust him for a new beginning.

That's exactly what Jonah did. In fact, much of his prayer spoke of his deliverance in the past tense—even though he was still contained within an enormous fish. That's faith. There's no reason to believe he wasn't genuinely contrite, though he certainly had enough motivation to get right with God. He may have been willing to drown, but wasting away in an animal's digestive system was an entirely different matter. He was ready to be delivered.

Desperate Prayer: Jonah 2:1–10

Jonah prays a profound prayer that is filled with all the right words. The fact that he is apparently fluent in the language of psalmistry is further proof that his theology is as straight as a prophet's should be. But that isn't the issue in Jonah's rebellion. It's his heart. His beliefs may be relatively in order, but his heart doesn't line up with the character of God. Where God is compassionate, Jonah isn't. That's why he's in the belly of a fish.

So Jonah cries out. The sailors have already shown some sort of repentance; the Ninevites are about to. In between, it's Jonah's turn. Though he never actually confesses his sin, he accurately assesses his situation—he's as low and hopeless as a guy can get—he reaffirms his commitment to the God of Israel, and he pledges certain sacrifices and vows. It's rather unlikely that he's interested in going to Nineveh yet, but from his newfound per-

JONAH'S PSALM

If the words of Jonah's prayer sound familiar, perhaps it's because much of it is a patchwork compilation from the Psalms. Compare:

Jonah	Psalm
2:2	18:6; 30:3
2:3	42:7
2:4	31:22
2:5	69:1–2; 18:4–5
2:6	40:2; 71:20; 88:6
2:7	18:6
2:8	31:6; 106:36
2:9	50:14; 66:13–14

It's even possible that this prayer, as Jonah has worded it, was a well-known psalm or hymn in its own right.

spective in the depths of the sea, Nineveh seems like the better option. So Jonah repents, and the fish regurgitates him at the shore. He lives to see another day—and hear another call.

Discuss

- Do you think Christians today are more interested in learning objective truths about God or in sharing his heart's desires? What leads you to that conclusion?

_____

_____

_____

_____

_____

- Would you consider Jonah's repentance genuine? Why or why not?

  _____

  _____

  _____

  _____

  _____

- How does your prayer life change when you're in a crisis? In what ways do seasons of hardship draw you closer to God?

  _____

  _____

  _____

  _____

  _____

Romans 1:18-25

A CASE STUDY

Imagine: You've lived most of your adult life in a luxury high-rise condo, but a couple of years ago, you thought you sensed God leading you to start an inner-city ministry for abandoned children. Though the idea intrigued you, the logistics were too hard to overcome. You would have had to quit your lucrative job, move into a high-crime area, adopt a more stringent standard of living, and work extremely long hours. You honestly didn't think you could adjust to the lifestyle. But you soon lost your lucrative job anyway when your company went bankrupt, and though you had no active role in the stock scandal that brought it down, the prosecutors did a good job of portraying you as negligent and, therefore, guilty by implication. Six months into your two-year prison term, you'd give anything be able to work freely at an inner-city ministry.

- Why does the prospect of a difficult, inconvenient task seem so unappealing from one perspective and so highly desirable from another?

- Is it possible for us to change our perspective without God putting us in situations that will force us to change it? If so, how?

- Have you ever sensed God's leading but then hardened yourself to it because of the difficult logistics involved? If so, what would God need to do in your life to cause you to reconsider?

Powerful Words

JONAH 3

"The end is near! Repent!" We can easily picture those words on a placard held by a scraggly-bearded hippie wearing a peace-sign T-shirt. And for most people, the connotations aren't very favorable. In certain eras, the message has been displayed frequently and prominently. It has rarely generated a positive reaction.

Repentance has gotten a bad rap. It's such a negative sounding word, even though the purpose and the outcome are remarkably positive. It's life-giving, in fact. Without repentance, we remain dead in our sins.

God's response to Jonah's disobedience is love. It's a tough love, to be sure, but it's sympathetic and unwavering. In fact, though both God and Jonah come across rather sternly in this book—Jonah much more so, of course—a discerning eye can see

23

God's deep and tender love at every turn. He spoke to a prophet because of his concern for people who had no knowledge of or interest in him—and, frankly, who had grossly perverted his ways for centuries. He refused to give up on Jonah, not because there was no one else to recruit, but because he wanted to share his heart with a prophet who needed to get the prejudice and anger out of his life. And he continues to teach Jonah even after Nineveh's repentance is secured. On every page, God is breathing his compassion on people.

God didn't require repentance of the Assyrians in order to humiliate them. He required it in order to preserve their lives. Turning away from sin and toward God may be painful initially, but so is childbirth. And both lead to something wonderful.

God's persistence with us may seem like an annoyance at times; we have a funny way of interpreting the conviction of his Spirit as nagging. But God doesn't point out our need for repentance in order to punish us. He points it out because judgment is the last thing he wants. We don't call him the God of second chances because he enjoys double failure. We call him that because he is constantly teaching and training, always preferring mercy over judgment, forever looking at our potential instead of our past. Whenever conviction seems unpleasant, remember that it leads to eternal pleasures (Ps. 16:11). God loves to set us up for his love.

Let's Try This Again: Jonah 3:1–5

The voice of God comes again to Jonah, and though it's essentially the same message, it's worded slightly differently. God had spelled it out a little more clearly the first time around: "Go to the great city of Nineveh and *preach against it*" (1:1). Now even more faith is required: "Go to the great city of Nineveh

A GREAT CITY

The Hebrew of 3:3 describes Nineveh as a very great city that would take three days to walk through. That's about a fifty-mile walk, and Nineveh was well under ten miles in diameter; so the description refers either to a very generous circumference or a thorough tour up and down the streets of the city. Some translations interpret the description in terms of significance rather than size; it's a "very important" city requiring a three-day visit—a length of stay consistent with diplomatic protocol of the time. Either way, whether a matter of size or significance, the city was the target of God's compassion—which would make it extremely important and certainly worthy of a very long stay.

and *proclaim to it the message I give you*" (3:1). In other words, the reiteration of the call will require Jonah to hear and preach his message on the spot rather than come up with some indicting words on the way. And this time, Jonah obeys.

There's nothing fancy about his sermon: "Forty more days and Nineveh will be overturned" (3:4). Though the implications seem clear on the surface, it's possible that God has given his servant a double message. "Overturned" generally means "overthrown," as in "destroyed"; but it can also simply mean "turned," as in "changed." Though Jonah certainly preaches it as a prediction of judgment, it can also be interpreted as a prophecy of repentance. Regardless, the prophet knows that he wouldn't be delivering this message if God only wanted to pour out his judgment on Assyrians. There's a contingency at play, an implicit invitation to repent in these words.

Remarkably, this dreaded enemy of Israel accepts the invitation. There's no hint of a lengthy explanation of why repentance might be necessary, no pleading and pulling on Ninevite heart-

FASTING ANIMALS?

It isn't often than livestock is portrayed as repentant (3:7–8). The king's proclamation that the beasts of Nineveh should join in the fast has fed plenty of speculation by commentators. Some assume that the writer made a blunder, but a simple oversight makes little sense in light of the emphatic repetition of the command. Some attribute the absurdity to the writer's playful sense of humor—a possibility if the story is interpreted as a parable, but hardly befitting a historical account. Much more likely is a rhetorical overstatement, a hyperbolism—a means of emphasizing comprehensive, meticulous repentance in every area of life. Imagine, for example, an office manager saying, "No one's going anywhere until we find that file, even if everyone in the building has to look for it—including the potted plants!" Ludicrous? Yes, but a very effective way to make a point. The king wanted the thorough involvement of all Ninevites in this collective change of heart.

strings, no extended altar calls. There's simply a warning and a powerful move of God that changes the hearts and minds of people who have not known him. Faith rises up in them and they turn from their wickedness.

Discuss

- Considering how uncomplicated the message was, why do you think God insisted on sending this particular prophet to preach it? What does his insistence tell us about his willingness to give us second chances in the aftermath of our rebellion?

_____

_____

_____

- Do you think God's plans change according to how human beings respond? Why or why not?

_____

_____

_____

A Small Seed with Enormous Fruit: Jonah 3:6–10

The king of Nineveh reacts immediately to the prophetic warning—not as one might expect, with vengeance and a prompt execution, but with genuine alarm and grief. Has word of the sailors' experience on the ship gotten all the way to Nineveh? Has the king had any previous experience with Israel's God that such fear should grip him? We don't know because the text doesn't say. All we know is that he hears of God's displeasure, and it terrifies him to the point that he calls for a rigorous and exhaustive repentance in every corner of the city.

God's response is as immediate as the king's. He sees what they have done—not what they believe or say or decide, but what they do—and his compassion is stirred. This isn't a conversion to Judaism, by any means; it's simply a decisive turning away from wickedness. So God relents from the judgment he would have poured out on them.

Discuss

- Have you ever seen a hardhearted person suddenly soften and grieve over sin? What prompted the change, and what did it look like?

_____

_____

_____

27

• Do you think repentance is always accompanied by outward evidence? Why or why not?

_____

_____

_____

_____

_____

_____

A CASE STUDY

Imagine: It was one of the most repressive governments on earth, forbidding even the foreign aid that came with no strings attached. Any kind of political speech was strictly forbidden, and economic activity was highly regulated. While the rest of the world was advancing and growing more independent in trade and technology, the citizens of this country seemed to have been stuck in a pre-industrial, agrarian world.

But global headlines one morning reported perhaps the most stunning policy reversal in history. Prompted by no protests, strikes, military action, assassination, or any other form of political unrest, the nation's leaders decided to abandon authoritarianism and begin establishing a free society. Pundits immediately assumed an economic motive, but local sources reported rumors of a religious movement sweeping the country.

- How likely or unlikely does this fictitious example seem to you? Why?

- Why do you think the media would likely focus more on natural economic and political explanations than spiritual explanations? Which reasons would you tend to focus on?

- Do you think God wants or plans to initiate national revivals in the future as he did with Nineveh? To what extent do you pray for him to do so?

The Message and the Messenger

JONAH 4

Long ago, one king wrote a message to send to the ruler of an offensive enemy kingdom. He sealed the message and gave it to one of his trusted couriers, who immediately began the dangerous ten-day journey to deliver it. Along the way, however, the messenger, who had long hoped his king would finally have the nerve to declare war on the enemy, became overwhelmed with curiosity and decided to unseal the letter. When he read it, he was stunned. Instead of the declaration of war he expected, it was a proposal for peace. He felt betrayed and even ashamed to deliver such an embarrassing token of weakness. He and his people would become a laughingstock, simply because an old king didn't have a backbone. After much thought, he decided to act in the best interests of the kingdom. He would bury the letter and return home with a well-crafted lie.

His plan was interrupted, however, when a group of scouts from the enemy kingdom discovered him burying the missive. They seized him—and the letter—and carried both back to their ruler's palace. Surprisingly the message delighted the rival king, and a peace treaty was soon forged. And with the kingdoms now being on friendly terms, the messenger was released unharmed. But he remained bitterly disappointed, disillusioned, and reluctant to call any place his home.

This, of course, is the basic story of Jonah recast in a different setting in order to focus on an important question: Who owns the message—the messenger or the author? Jonah obviously felt a certain right to refuse to deliver the message he was called to preach, even though it was never his message to begin with. He didn't approve of it and wanted no part in it. His own King was essentially issuing an invitation to make peace with Israel's dreaded enemy—the same enemy that had periodically wreaked havoc on Israel's borders and committed crimes against its people. This didn't seem at all like the God he thought he knew.

With the danger of dying at the hands of Assyrians no longer a factor, the reasons for the prophet's initial disobedience are more clearly exposed. His flight to Tarshish had been more than self-preservation; it was a matter of moral outrage. Jonah begins to speak as though he is on higher moral ground than the God who called him.

At Odds with God: Jonah 4:1–4

Most preachers are elated when people respond to their message. But Jonah isn't like most preachers, and the people he addresses are not like any he's ever preached to. They are not, and

JONAH'S LAMENT

The prophet's description of God—apparently the divine source of his misery—is more than a random collection of adjectives. It's a virtual quote of Exodus 34:6–7, God's description of himself when he let Moses see his glory. Jonah is essentially complaining that because of God's true nature, he knew his message of judgment had a non-judgmental purpose behind it—that the ultimate goal was repentance. And the last thing cruel Ninevites should receive, according to the prophet's sentiments, was mercy—especially while Israel was so frequently under God's heavy discipline for the idolatry and injustices of her kings. Jonah might as well have said, "I know your Name, and these people don't deserve it!"

will never be, friends of Israel. He has lived his entire life in a culture that breeds animosity against its hostile enemies—and not without reason. Israel had experienced Assyria's raids in the past. The prophet's righteous indignation is hard to reconcile with the mercy of God.

Jonah's indignation is not much different than that of another prophet. Habakkuk relentlessly questioned God over the seeming injustice of punishing his own people by using a far more corrupt nation: Babylon. But the similarities between the two prophets end when God explains his intentions to each. Habakkuk praises God for his righteousness, even though he doesn't completely understand it. Jonah is eaten up with bitterness—so much so that he asks for God to take his life.

Not only has Jonah missed God's compassion, but he also has forgotten that Assyria's repentance would be an enormous blessing for Israel. A docile, godly enemy-turned-friend is better than an aggressive, die-hard foe. The principle is that God's people are never isolated from the world they live in. When

FEELING DECEIVED

Jonah prophesied destruction, and destruction never came. From all outward appearances, that's a false prophecy—and, if anyone back in Israel heard about it, the end of a good career. Though the penalties of Deuteronomy 18:20 (death for false prophets) were rarely carried out during most of Israel's history, the stigma would remain. Jonah's word would forever be suspiciously unreliable. That embarrassment, added to his animosity for Assyrians, was enough to make Jonah "greatly displeased" with God's treatment of him. His desires, his reputation, and his opinion were completely bypassed in the prophetic process. But on that count, he would find himself in good company with a later prophet. Jeremiah once felt almost exactly the same way (Jer. 20:7).

God's blessings fall on the ungodly, the godly benefit too—and vice versa. The sun rises and the rain falls for both the righteous and the wicked (Matt. 5:45). For a nation to be at peace with its enemies, its enemies have to be peaceful. Jonah's preaching could have spared Israel from an impending calamity.

Discuss

- If God is the author of the gospel, and we're its messengers, how much latitude do you think we have in determining when and where to deliver it? Other than with the words he spoke, how could Jonah have further demonstrated God's message to Nineveh?

_____

_____

_____

_____

34

- In what situation(s) have you found yourself at odds with God?

  _____

  _____

  _____

  _____

  _____

Object Lesson: Jonah 4:5–10

How does God respond? by giving Jonah an object lesson in a helpful vine he hadn't asked for. As the prophet is fuming over the repentant city and this travesty of justice, God gives him extra shade to shelter him from the sun. The next morning, a worm eats away at the vine and causes it to wither, and a scorching wind beats against Jonah. This stirs up further anger, but God has made his point. The "man of God"—a frequent designation for a prophet—values his own immediate comfort much more than he values thousands of enemy lives. His ethnocentric focus has blinded him to the heart of his Lord.

Jonah is the most effective prophet in the Bible. He runs from God, and sailors are converted. He goes reluctantly to Nineveh with a five-word sermon (in Hebrew), and an evil city repents. He bitterly pouts over a withered vine, and the compassion of God is revealed in a prophetic book to a chosen but apostate nation. The irony is that Isaiah and Jeremiah spilled their lives out with many words over unhearing, unrepentant people and would have rejoiced to see even a hint of fruitfulness. Jonah sees fruitfulness in spite of himself, and he hates it.

Even then, God's compassion toward his prophet is relentless. He doesn't disown his disgruntled servant. He patiently and persistently absorbs Jonah's anger, hears his questions, and even answers them. He does with Jonah what he has already done with Nineveh. He reveals his heart.

In fact, that's how the book concludes. "Should I not be concerned about that great city?" the Lord asks. It's a rhetorical question that leaves readers with a decision to make. Are we in sync with our Creator's desires? Can we get on board with the big picture of his purposes? Will we align our hearts with the missionary heart of God?

Discuss

- In what ways can bitterness skew our perspective of God? What does Jonah's experience tell us about how people with deeply rooted bitterness over the circumstances of their lives can find healing for their pain?

  _____

  _____

  _____

  _____

  _____

- To what extent do you think Christians live by an "us-and-them" mentality? In what ways does this attitude hinder God's work in your community? In the world?

  _____

  _____

  _____

  _____

  _____

A Case Study

Imagine: It's 1946, and your London neighborhood still bears the marks of Nazi bombs. Worse than that, so does your soul. You lost several relatives during the war, including your only brother. You know intellectually that only a small but persuasive sector of German society was responsible for the war, but the bitterness in your heart extends to all German-speaking people. You'd prefer to keep your distance for the rest of your life. The problem is that your work puts you in close contact with quite a few Germans who are also recovering from the war and clearly need God's love. And while most were innocent bystanders in the conflict, some were instigators of it. Seeing them every day is difficult. Forgiving them seems impossible.

- What do you think God would want to say to the Germans you work with? In what ways is it different than what you would like to say to them?
- When we notice a discrepancy between God's perspective and ours, what can we do to synchronize with him?
- If God told you to deliver his message of forgiveness to the person toward whom you feel most angry and bitter, how would you respond? Why?

A Changed Life

JOEL 2:12–13; 2 CHRONICLES 7:14; MATTHEW 4:17

Three friends ran a side business together, selling prescription painkillers illegally to people who needed them. Well, most of their clients needed them. Or maybe some did. Anyway, it was a very profitable business, and it seemed to be running smoothly and staying under the radar of local law enforcement.

One day, one of their oldest clients—an influential woman who had been buying from them since her surgery years ago— informed them that she would no longer be needing their services. She had "got religion," it seemed, and decided that the chronic indulgence of her addiction didn't fit her character anymore. She also strongly suggested—some might call it preaching—that they get out of their sordid business. "The

Lord wouldn't be pleased with it," she told them. "It enslaves too many lives." And that was the last they heard of her.

The three friends reacted differently to this turn of events. They all, of course, began to wonder if she would turn them in, so their conscience and a fair amount of paranoia seemed to follow them constantly now. But beyond that, they each had a different take on the ex-client's words. One of the friends decided that the lady was exactly right—they *were* doing something unethical, perhaps even morally wrong. He understood their sin, but he was strongly tempted by the profits. So he stayed in the game.

The second friend started to feel guilty. He couldn't really explain *why* their activity was wrong—after all, they weren't forcing anyone to buy their drugs—but his conscience was un-

THE REST OF THE STORY

Nineveh's repentance didn't dramatically change the course of its history, at least from a purely human perspective. About a generation after Jonah's ministry, the Assyrian Empire (for which Nineveh served as the capital) overthrew the northern kingdom of Israel and took over the region of Samaria. The typical Assyrian practice was to assimilate conquered people among its own citizens, eroding the culture and national identity of the vanquished. For that reason, the ten tribes of the north were interspersed and intermarried with Assyrians, dispersed across the empire, and robbed of their distinctiveness—one reason that Jews in the time of Jesus considered Samaritans to be loathsome half-breeds.

After flourishing for another few decades after Samaria's defeat—and besieging Jerusalem during the time of King Hezekiah—Assyria began to lose power. The prophet Nahum spoke God's judgment against Nineveh in the mid-600s BC, and this time there was no repentance. The city was overthrown in 612.

settled. He was truly sorry if he had harmed anyone. He felt as if he wanted to stop. But the pressure not to let his friends down got the best of him. He kept at it too.

The third friend didn't think there was anything wrong with their business, and he didn't want to quit it. But for some reason, the lady's words stuck. Reluctantly, he pulled out. He didn't even know why. He just didn't want to take any chances with God.

Which of the friends repented? Technically, none of them did. Complete repentance would have incorporated the reactions of all three. For repentance to be real and lasting, it has to involve one's mind, heart, and actions. Understanding the need without doing anything about it is hypocrisy. Wanting to repent but never following through on it is either apathy or cowardice. And behavior modification without any change of heart results in empty ritualism. None are what God desires. Repentance as God intends it is a changed mind, a changed heart, and changed behavior. That's the kind of repentance that, according to three parables in Luke 15, causes great joy in heaven.

The Ninevites seemed to have repented thoroughly. Outside of biblical history, there's no evidence that it lasted beyond a generation, or even that it happened at all. But Scripture is clear that God moved among them. They changed their minds, hearts, and actions in turning from their wickedness. And God withheld his wrath.

"Repentability": Joel 2:12–13

Few people enjoy being confronted with their mistakes. In fact, most of us will become defensive in such confrontations, not because we believe we're guilt free, but because we're offended that someone had the audacity to point out our flaws. It's a

41

THE DAY OF ATONEMENT

Yom Kippur—the Day of Atonement prescribed in Leviticus 23:26–32—is the holiest day on the Jewish calendar, the "Sabbath of all Sabbaths." It's a time of fasting and intense introspection to identify and confess any sins of the previous year. It is traditionally the day that foreshadows the final judgment when God determines each person's fate. In biblical times, it was the one day of the year when the high priest entered the Holy of Holies to atone for the sins of the nation and when a scapegoat was sent into the desert to bear away Israel's sins (Leviticus 16). The primary purpose of the observance then and now is to make peace with God. It begins solemnly and ends with a sense of release.

Synagogue services on Yom Kippur last all day, but the afternoon service is particularly relevant to our study. The book of Jonah is read out loud in its entirety as an example of true repentance. It's a remarkable statement that the pattern held high on Judaism's holiest day of the year is the repentance of an ancient Gentile enemy. Even more remarkable in that example is the relentless compassion of God.

natural reaction. The problem is that Scripture rarely tells us simply to act naturally—at least according to our old nature. We're supposed to act out of the new nature we've been supernaturally endowed with.

Scripture is overflowing with calls to repentance. Ever since the fall in Eden, God has been calling his people to reject their sinful nature and turn to him. Joel 2:12–13 is a small but representative sampling of that call. The book of Jonah is another. And in every case, a sign of spiritual maturity is the responsiveness—the "repentability"—of those who recognize their sin.

Who responds according to God's desires in the book of Jonah? Gentile sailors and an enemy's capital city. Who doesn't?

A chosen prophet from a chosen nation. The story oozes with irony, as the "ungodly" nation turns to God while the "godly" prophet turns away and sulks. Jonah has demonstrated little repentance except when under the pressure of being potential fish food. When allowed to express his true heart, his pride and bitterness show up clearly.

Discuss

- In 2 Samuel 12:1–14, David does not get defensive when he is confronted with his sin. How well do you think Christians follow his model of humble confession? How well do you?

_____

_____

_____

_____

_____

A Joint Venture: 2 Chronicles 7:14

God deals with each of us as individuals. He also deals with us corporately. He promised that if his people—together—united in their remorse and confession of sins, he would forgive them and heal their land. Though it isn't an exact social science, history has shown that, in general, when a nation's leaders and its people turn away from wickedness and embrace righteous ways, social and economic problems usually begin to resolve. Their turning doesn't create instant prosperity or eliminate all unrest, but it does foster stability and growth. God's promise to heal nations has been experienced by many.

43

Discuss

- To what extent have you thought of repentance as a united, collective response to God?

  _____

  _____

  _____

  _____

- How do you think God blesses individuals who turn to him? Do the same blessings apply to families? Churches? Cities? Nations?

  _____

  _____

  _____

  _____

First Things First: Matthew 4:17

The first message Jesus preached was the same message John the Baptist was known for: "Repent, for the kingdom of heaven is near." That's because the ability to hear his voice and accept his words often requires a change in thinking, a change of heart, and a change in behavior—which is essentially what repentance is. Those who are content in the status quo, stubborn in their ways, and/or attached to their sins will not even have "ears to hear" the gospel. That applies not only to unbelievers but also to Christians. It's entirely possible for believers to get so stuck in their ways that they miss the leadings and movements of the Spirit. So before any other sermon or miracle, Jesus began his ministry with the fundamental prerequisite: repent.

Discuss

• In what ways does repentance serve as a blessing in our lives? Why do you think most people see this blessing as an unpleasant chore or offensive requirement?

_____

_____

_____

_____

_____

A Case Study

Imagine: A young, outspoken teacher speaks at your church one Sunday, and initially you're impressed. But as his message progresses and his enthusiasm builds, his words get harsher. This generation, he contends, has grossly corrupted biblical truth, and God isn't pleased. By the time he's done, your members—and Christians in general—have been raked over the coals for getting caught up in the culture's materialism, indecencies, and injustices. And, seeing the look on your faces, he marvels that your church doesn't cry out for forgiveness on the spot—just as churches did in the days of Jonathan Edwards and George Whitefield in the 1700s. What began as a friendly exhortation has turned into an extremely blunt call to either repent or be disciplined by the mighty hand of God.

- How well do you think your congregation would receive such a message? How well would you?
- Would you dispute his contention that Christians are often influenced too much by the sins of the culture? Why or why not?
- Why do you think messages like "repent" always, even in Jesus's day, have seemed so acceptable in the past but so offensive in the present?

The Sign of Jonah

MATTHEW 12:39–42; LEVITICUS 16

Joe is in his element. He loves going to missions conferences, and his church's annual event is always done right. He looks forward to tasting the variety of ethnic foods missionaries offer at their display tables, hearing different languages spoken, and picturing himself in other places absorbing interesting cultures. Most of all, he enjoys hearing stories of how God is touching lives overseas and calling more and more people to foreign fields. His heart is always stirred to give more money, pray more prayers, and even go on more trips. After all, people around the world are dying without Christ. The Great Commission simply *has* to be fulfilled. To Joe, this is more than every Christian's responsibility. It's his God-given passion.

47

JONAH AND AHAB

"If we obey God, we must disobey ourselves; and it is in this disobeying ourselves, wherein the hardness of obeying God consists." So says Father Mapple, the preacher whose sermon Captain Ahab's crew listens to before going whaling. Author Herman Melville had a good model for Ahab when he wrote *Moby Dick*: the prophet Jonah. Like Jonah, Ahab is bitter and obsessed with "justice." He is relentlessly angry at an elusive whale whose ways are mysterious and uncontainable, just as Jonah is angry at the God whose ways he doesn't understand and who seems dangerous (and fishy) to those who try to tame his plans. Though we have no idea how Jonah's life went after his Nineveh mission, the text leaves us with the impression that he'd be a lot like Ahab: still wrestling obsessively with issues much bigger than himself.

When the conference ends on Sunday night, Joe goes home to get a good night's sleep. He gets up early Monday morning, as he always does, and drinks his first cup of coffee as he and his wife peruse the newspaper. But when his wife reads a blurb in the local news section, he's jolted awake before his coffee can take effect. It seems that the city's Muslim population is growing, spreading further into the suburbs—and one group has announced plans to build a mosque less than a mile from their house.

"What!?" Joe exclaims. "Do you realize what that will do to our property value?"

"Well, I'm sure you can get the neighborhood association to petition against rezoning," she answers.

"I will. We have to!" Joe takes another sip of his coffee and shakes his head. "Man, there goes the neighborhood."

There's a lot of zeal among Christians for sharing the glorious truth of the gospel with the rest of the world. But evangelistic fervor that burns bright on a theoretical level, like Joe's, is often quenched in the trenches of real life and can lead people with good intentions to say and do unthoughtful things.

That's how it was with first-century Judaism too. The religious leaders who opposed Jesus so strongly knew well that God had given Jews the distinct honor of being a light to the nations (Isa. 51:4; 60:3), and they rejoiced in the privilege. Many of them even sought converts among the Gentiles by funding ambassadors for their faith (see Matthew 23:15 for Jesus's opinion on that). But when Jesus remarked on how Elijah and Elisha found more responsiveness among Gentiles than among Jews, his opponents were furious (Luke 4:25–27). Jesus was implying that the current generation of Jews was just as unresponsive as those in the times of the kings. So Jesus ministered to a Roman centurion, a Gadarene demoniac, a Syro-Phoenician woman, and plenty of other Gentiles in the northern fringes of Galilee. And he insisted that many non-Jews would come to God's banquet from every direction while many Jews from Israel would be excluded (Luke 13:28–29).

In Matthew 12:18–21, Jesus quotes a passage from Isaiah that foretells his ministry to the nations (Isa. 42:1–4). And a few verses later (12:39–41), he invokes the example of Jonah. It's a loaded image with echoes of sacrifice, redemption, a descent into the earth, and a massive ingathering of unlikely pagans. When Jesus speaks of the sign of Jonah, he preaches several messages at once.

Symbol: Matthew 12:39–42

Jesus's reference to the sign of Jonah is meant to draw attention to his forthcoming resurrection. As Jonah was in the dark depths for three days and nights and was then brought back into the

ISRAEL AND THE SEA

Phoenicians were the best sailors of the ancient world. Jews were at the other end of the spectrum. In Jewish thought, the sea represented chaos and crisis, darkness and danger, the mysterious and murky deep. Not only does that concept shed further light on the disciples' terror during a storm, but it also shows Jonah's flight from Joppa to be even more desperate than it appears on the surface. Jonah would rather take his chances in oblivion than minister to godless Assyrians.

That's a symbolic picture of God's people when we stand between a radical call and assimilation into our culture. We're faced with a choice between tumultuous waters and heroic faith. Like Jonah, many believers choose the turmoil of the sea and then must be pushed into God's will for their lives. Jesus willingly chose his mission—three days of death and a relentless pursuit of hopeless people. In many respects, he calls us to do the same.

light of life, so will Jesus soon be entombed for three days and nights and then be raised to glory, after which multitudes of Gentiles will hear God's voice and repent. The three-day theme is echoed throughout Jewish history, from the ninth plague on Egypt (three days in darkness) to the teachings of Kabbalah (Jewish mysticism) that Jonah actually died and was resurrected in his three days in the water.

Jesus's point in identifying the sign of Jonah is that Nineveh repented after a one-line sermon from a stubborn prophet, and the Jewish leaders listening to Jesus's extensive teachings will not. His contemporaries are a hardhearted and evil generation, he says. There's irony in that observation: the Ninevites were wicked non-Jews, and the Jewish leaders consider themselves "the chosen ones." Yet Jesus is clear about which group is more spiritually responsive and, therefore, pleasing to God.

His audience, he implies, is more hard-headed than a bunch of Assyrians.

Jesus has another, more subtle, point of similarity with Jonah. It was supposed during the times of both Jonah and Jesus that God's agenda, as gleaned from prophecy and national pride, was to glorify himself in the visible victory of his people over ungodly and oppressive kingdoms. As it turns out, Jesus's mission, like Jonah's, is a spiritual battle that will end in a victory of conversion rather than subjugation. Neither Rome nor Assyria would be conquered by Israel's army. The triumph would come in the inner workings of human hearts.

Discuss

- Many of Israel's prophets did miracles. How does "the sign of Jonah" distinguish Jesus as unique and serve as the singular mark of authenticity to his generation?

_____

_____

_____

_____

Sacrifice: Leviticus 16:7–10

Leviticus 16 offers a dramatic picture of salvation. On the annual Day of Atonement, Israel's high priest would select a goat, impart all the sins of the nation onto it, and drive the sin-laden animal far out into the desert. The prophetic image portrays judgment falling on the sacrifice instead of the nation.

That's where we get the term "scapegoat," and that's essentially what Jonah became when he was on his ship. By being sacrificed—thrown into the water—judgment was averted. The storm of wrath immediately calmed, as one man bore punishment for the safety of all others on board. Though Jonah's punishment was deserved, his ability to avert God's wrath away from the sailors and onto himself points us to another servant of God who bore the wrath for the sake of others. This servant was entirely innocent, but he was entombed in the depths for three days so the rest of us wouldn't have to go down with the ship. When Jesus died on the cross, the storm of wrath subsided. Our Scapegoat saw the light again after three days, and like Jonah did, he leads sinners to repentance.

Discuss

- How do the sailors' attempts to save the ship (1:11–13) compare to our attempts at salvation? How does their response to Jonah as a scapegoat (1:16) compare to our response to Jesus as the Scapegoat?

  _____

  _____

  _____

  _____

- What kinds of spiritual responsiveness do you think God sees in our generation? As a whole, are we more like Jonah, the sailors, the Ninevites, or the Jewish leaders of Jesus's day?

  _____

  _____

  _____

  _____

A Case Study

Imagine: Like Joe in the introduction to this session, you enjoy talking about missions, giving and praying for missions, and going on mission trips. One year on a trip to a remote village, you witness the immediate conversion of an entire tribe. And even though this tribe has never been discipled or studied the Bible, their effortless prayers result in dramatic miracles, and their worship seems more genuine than anything you've ever experienced—all within their first week of being believers. And some of them even begin to take it upon themselves to instruct you in the ways of the Lord.

- What emotions would this reversal of expected roles between your mission team and the locals cause you to have? Why?
- What advice would you give to these villagers about growing in the Lord? About evangelizing other villages? About how to conduct a church service?
- Why do you think God sometimes moves dramatically and swiftly among one group of people while working slowly and thoroughly with another? Which would you rather experience, and why?

Conclusion

Disobedience and repentance. Judgment and mercy. The will of God and the ways of humanity. These are the tense moments in Jonah, a message that seems very well-attuned with the fears and biases of our hearts. But these forty-eight verses of Scripture not only call us to a vision larger than ourselves; they offer us a glimpse of our Creator's compassionate heart. More than that, they invite us to share his purposes, to saturate ourselves in his ways, to think and to feel his mercy.

Jonah is a great example of how we can be completely orthodox in our beliefs and yet heretical in our behavior. For most of the book, he says all the right words but does all the wrong things. And though he doesn't show us what blessings an enthusiastic prophet would have gained from boldly declaring God's word among those who don't know him, the rest of the Bible does. The New Testament is full of stories of both the hardships and rewards that come from serving God with reckless abandon. So is Christian history. And the rewards are always greater. Those who demonstrate God's relentless grace in the way they live will find themselves experiencing his grace in greater and greater measure.

Leader's Notes

Session 1

Jonah 1:1–3. The implication that Jonah may have chartered the entire boat is questionable, so it isn't worth basing much discussion on that assumption. But this possibility is clearly noted in some rabbinic commentaries. The NIV translation of verse 3 says: "After paying the fare...." The Hebrew text literally reads: "He paid its hire...." Jewish commentary also notes that it was not customary to pay a fare or a charter fee in advance, but Jonah was zealous enough about leaving that he gladly made the transaction before leaving port.

Session 3

Jonah 3:1–5, second discussion question. This issue of whether God changes his mind, so to speak, could turn into a lengthy discussion that takes up the whole session. For scriptural evidence, read the examples of Genesis 6:6, when God was grieved that he made the earth and decided to destroy humanity; and of God relenting from a plan after Moses asked him to in Exodus 32:7–14. On the other side of the issue, read Numbers 23:19, which clearly states that God does not change his mind. These passages won't resolve the issue, but they will demonstrate that the Bible holds these truths in tension. God's overall, sovereign plan doesn't change because his foreknowledge isn't lacking. His interaction with his people, however, is very often conditional.

Session 4

Jonah 4:5-10. In all likelihood, at least two or three people in your group wrestle with bitterness over some past offense—and perhaps even toward God. If these feelings come to the surface, allow them to be freely expressed and use the opportunity for other group members to encourage and pray for the healing of past wounds. Group support and affirmation can powerfully unravel bitterness in a person's life.

Session 5

2 Chronicles 7:14. Some participants in your discussion may be able to think of examples of how repentance on a large scale affects social structures. If there's time, you may want to discuss the implications of 2 Chronicles 7:14 for your country.

Bibliography

Berlin, Adele, Marc Zvi Brettler, and Michael Fishbane, eds. *The Jewish Study Bible*. Oxford and New York: Oxford University Press, 2004.

Chilton, Bruce, et al. *The Cambridge Companion to the Bible*. Cambridge and New York: Cambridge University Press, 1997.

Colson, Chuck, et al., eds. *The Apologetics Study Bible*. Nashville: Holman, 2007.

Craigie, Peter C. *Twelve Prophets*. Volume 1. Louisville: Westminster John Knox Press, 1984.

Dumbrell, William J. *The Faith of Israel: A Theological Survey of the Old Testament*. Grand Rapids: Baker Academic, 2002.

Hoerth, Alfred J. *Archaeology and the Old Testament*. Grand Rapids: Baker Books, 1998.

Kaiser, Walter C., Jr., and Duane Garrett, eds. *Archaeological Study Bible*. Grand Rapids: Zondervan, 2006.

Rosenberg, A. J., ed. *The Twelve Prophets*, Volume 1. New York: Judaica Press, 1986.

Ryken, Leland, and Philip Graham Ryken, eds. *The Literary Study Bible*. Wheaton, IL: Crossway, 2007.

Shanks, Herschel, ed. *Ancient Israel: From Abraham to the Roman Destruction of the Temple.* Upper Saddle River, NJ: Prentice Hall, 1999.

Sproul, R. C., and Keith Mathison, eds. *The Reformation Study Bible.* Phillipsburg, NJ: P&R Publishing, 2005.

Telushkin, Joseph. *Biblical Literacy: The Most Important People, Events, and Ideas of the Hebrew Bible.* New York: William Morrow, 1997.

Walton, John H., and Andrew E. Hill. *The Old Testament Today: A Journey from Original Meaning to Contemporary Significance.* Grand Rapids: Zondervan, 2004.

Walton, John H., Victor H. Matthews, and Mark W. Chavalas. *The IVP Bible Background Commentary: Old Testament.* Downers Grove, IL: InterVarsity Press, 2000.

Wilkinson, Bruce, and Kenneth Boa. *Talk Thru the Old Testament.* Nashville: Thomas Nelson, 1983.

**WALK
THRU THE
BIBLE®**

Helping people everywhere
live God's Word

For more than three decades, Walk Thru the Bible has created discipleship materials and cultivated leadership networks that together are reaching millions of people through live seminars, print publications, audiovisual curricula, and the Internet. Known for innovative methods and high-quality resources, we serve the whole body of Christ across denominational, cultural, and national lines. Through our strong and cooperative international partnerships, we are strategically positioned to address the church's greatest need: developing mature, committed, and spiritually reproducing believers.

Walk Thru the Bible communicates the truths of God's Word in a way that makes the Bible readily accessible to anyone. We are committed to developing user-friendly resources that are Bible centered, of excellent quality, life changing for individuals, and catalytic for churches, ministries, and movements; and we are committed to maintaining our global reach through strategic partnerships while adhering to the highest levels of integrity in all we do.

Walk Thru the Bible partners with the local church worldwide to fulfill its mission, helping people "walk thru" the Bible with greater clarity and understanding. Live seminars and small group curricula are taught in over 45 languages by more than 80,000 people in more than 70 countries, and more than 100 million devotionals have been packaged into daily magazines, books, and other publications that reach over five million people each year.

Walk Thru the Bible
4201 North Peachtree Road
Atlanta, GA 30341-1207
770-458-9300
www.walkthru.org

Read the entire Bible in one year, thanks to the systematic reading plan in the best-selling **Daily Walk** devotional.

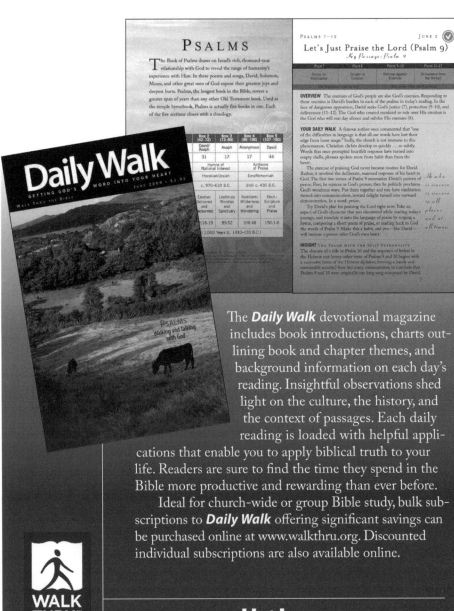

The **Daily Walk** devotional magazine includes book introductions, charts outlining book and chapter themes, and background information on each day's reading. Insightful observations shed light on the culture, the history, and the context of passages. Each daily reading is loaded with helpful applications that enable you to apply biblical truth to your life. Readers are sure to find the time they spend in the Bible more productive and rewarding than ever before.

Ideal for church-wide or group Bible study, bulk subscriptions to **Daily Walk** offering significant savings can be purchased online at www.walkthru.org. Discounted individual subscriptions are also available online.

WALK THRU THE BIBLE

www.walkthru.org